D1020675

Careers for

TECH GIRLS IN VIDEO GAME DEVELOPMENT

LAURA LA BELLA

ROSEN PUBLISHING

New York

Published in 2016 by The Rosen Publishing Group, Inc.
29 East 21st Street, New York, NY 10010

Copyright © 2016 by The Rosen Publishing Group, Inc.

First Edition

Library of Congress Cataloging-in-Publication Data

La Bella, Laura, author.
Careers for tech girls in video game development/Laura La Bella.—First edition.
         pages cm.—(Tech girls)
Includes bibliographical references and index.
ISBN 978-1-4994-6107-7 (library bound)
  1. Video games industry—Vocational guidance—Juvenile literature. 2. Video games—Design—
Vocational guidance—Juvenile literature. 3. Computer games—Design—Vocational guidance—
Juvenile literature. 4. Computer games—Programming—Vocational guidance—Juvenile literature.
[1. Vocational guidance.] I. Title.
GV1469.3.L32 2016
794.8023—dc23
                                                                                    2014045474

Manufactured in the United States of America

CONTENTS

Introduction

Halo is a best-selling military/science fiction shooting game that puts you behind the scope of a rifle as you fight in an interstellar war between humanity and an alliance of aliens known as the Covenant. Its executive producer is a woman named Kiki Wolfkill.

Wolfkill served as director of art at Microsoft Game Studios before taking control of *Halo* when Microsoft launched 343 Industries, a company created to manage and develop the *Halo* franchise. Wolfkill helped create *Halo 4: Forward Unto Dawn* and managed and produced *Halo: Nightfall*. She directs her team in programming and development, storytelling and scripting, and art direction and animation for the entire *Halo* franchise—a franchise that is worth big money. *Halo 4* grossed $220 million globally on the day it was launched. Within twenty-four hours, more than one million people had played the game.

Wolfkill is among a small but growing number of female video game developers, designers, programmers, producers, and writers who are changing the face of the gaming industry. For decades, there has been a lack of representation of female developers and designers in gaming. There has also been a lack of meaningful female characters within games. The characters that did exist were often in the

Kiki Wolfkill, the executive producer of the *Halo* franchise, has been named one of the most powerful women in gaming by *Fortune* magazine. Not only is she the brains behind *Halo*, but she also spearheaded the media cross-over of the game, which includes novels, comic books, and a web series.

background or were overly sexualized, unrealistic representations of women. This treatment was the direct result of a male-dominated industry where men were the creators, developers, and writers of video games. As of 2014, 48 percent of gamers are female, and women like Wolfkill are becoming key players in the industry.

According to the International Game Developers Association, the number of female developers working in the video game industry has doubled since 2009. Today, 22 percent of video game developers are female and are challenging the traditional fanboy culture that has ruled gaming. The growth is attributed to greater outreach to young women to make them aware of career opportunities in science, technology, engineering, and mathematics, or STEM. In 2009, the White House began a campaign to promote STEM education. Two of the people they selected to be part of the campaign were Sally Ride, the first American woman in space, and Ursula Burns, CEO of Xerox, indicating that the campaign would equally focus on girls and boys.

Even though women are behind the design and development of some of the industry's most popular games, they still remain, to some extent, outsiders in the gaming industry. Many female developers and designers experience harassment at work, online, and at conventions. Others report that they are viewed as less knowledgeable than their male counterparts. Nevertheless, the industry is beginning to change as more women seek employment in gaming. Gaming companies are recognizing the importance of women and their contributions to creating games. With women making up almost half of all gamers, companies are seeking out female employees to design and develop games that will appeal to women, young and old.

Today, some of the most popular games in the world, from *League of Legends, Skylanders: Giants,* and *N*, are developed and designed by women. Gaming is a dynamic, exciting industry that is growing in sales and in job opportunities. Careers in the industry are varied, and young women with an interest in design, development, and programming can build a rewarding career.

Chapter one

THE DYNAMIC GAMING INDUSTRY

I n September 2013, the video gaming industry reached a significant milestone when the four-teenth installment of *Grand Theft Auto*, an action-based, role-playing game where participants choose missions to steal cars and other items in order to rise through the ranks of a criminal organization, made more than $800 million in worldwide sales in its first twenty-four hours. That was the biggest launch day to date for any piece of entertainment, including films, DVD sales, and music. *Call of Duty: Black Ops 2*, a military-style, first-person shooting game, made $1 billion in fifteen days. By comparison, it took *Avatar*, the highest grossing Hollywood film so far in history, two days longer to hit the same goal.

A GAMING EXPERIENCE FOR EVERYONE

With a variety of games in a wide span of genres—from action-adventure games such as *Halo*, *World of Warcraft,* and *Gran Turismo* to community-building games such as *Farmville* and *Castleville* to puzzle/strategy/skill games like *Angry Birds* and *Candy Crush*—there is a gaming experience for everyone. And now, smartphones and mobile devices mean that you don't need a game console to be a gamer. Overall, 68 percent of gamers play on consoles such as the Sony PlayStation or Nintendo Wii, 53 percent play on smartphones, and 41 percent play on wireless devices like a tablet. Many games are multiplatform, which means you can play the same game on more than one device. You can begin playing a game on your personal computer and pick up playing where you left off on your smartphone or tablet or vice versa.

According to "The State of Gaming 2014," an annual overview of gaming industry trends, more than 48 million people play games on their smartphones or mobile devices.

According to fastcompany.com, the video game industry is projected to grow from $67 billion in 2013 to $82 billion in 2017. In the United States, 59 percent, or 186 million people, play games online, on their smartphones or mobile devices, or via game consoles in their homes.

A DIVERSE RANGE OF CAREER PATHS

An exciting aspect to a career in gaming and game development is the diverse range of careers available. Game development teams are made up of game designers and developers, programmers, production staff, audio experts, writers and storytellers, visual artists and illustrators, and business professionals in finance, marketing, and management. Each role contributes to the success of a game.

GAME DESIGNERS

Game designers are the visionaries behind games. They design characters, plots, and storylines, and decide how players interact with the game.

GAME PROGRAMMERS

Using lines of code and different programming languages that depend on whether the game will be played online, via a game console, or on a mobile device, game programmers control the game's environment, how players interact with one another, and how artwork and graphics are incorporated into a game.

AUDIO ENGINEERS AND SOUND DESIGNERS

All of the sounds you hear in a game, including background noises, music, and the sound used in play such as characters' voices, footfalls, traffic, or gun fire, are the job of an audio engineer or sound designer. These professionals are tasked with using sound to add dimension to a game.

VISUAL ARTISTS AND ILLUSTRATORS

These artists create the visual world of a game with illustration and graphics. From the colors and textures of buildings, the design of vehicles, and the look of characters and their clothing to the physical world (a city, a medieval kingdom, or outer space) in which the game is set are all the responsibility of the visual artists and illustrators.

PRODUCTION MANAGERS AND PRODUCERS

Producers and production managers keep the team on target for deadlines in the development of a project, support their team members, and ensure the game is being developed according to the project's specifications.

MANAGEMENT, MARKETING, AND FINANCE

Managers, marketing professionals, and financial experts oversee the business side of games. They coordinate the launch of new games, set pricing, oversee a gaming company's financial responsibilities, and market games to consumers.

WHERE THE GIRLS ARE

The 2014 survey "Essential Facts About the Computer and Video Game Industry," conducted by the Entertainment Software Association, revealed that of the 186 million video game players in the United States, 48 percent are women and girls. The survey also noted that women eighteen years of age and

Roberta Williams is the game designer who created *Phantasmagoria*. At the time of its launch, in 1995, it was hailed as one of the most ambitious computer games of all time.

older represent a significantly greater portion of the game-playing population than boys age eighteen and younger. While there are significant numbers of female gamers, there are fewer women involved in the industry as video game developers and designers.

Women have had a presence in the video gaming industry since the 1970s. Carol Shaw created a digital polo game as part of a marketing campaign for clothing designer Ralph Lauren. She also created the first commercially released game designed by a woman, *3-D Tic-Tac-Toe*, designed for Atari in 1980. Later, Shaw designed *River Raid* for Activision in 1983. In the 1980s, Dona Bailey was a programmer on *Centipede*, and Roberta Williams wrote games such as *King's Quest*, which pioneered the use of animation and environments that allowed characters to walk behind objects onscreen.

Despite the large number of female gamers, only 22 percent of game developers are women. Emily Taylor, a producer for the games *EverQuest Next* and *Landmark*, was interviewed in June 2014 by the *Los Angeles Times* and addressed the lack of women in gaming. "In my experience, I didn't realize that there was such a thing as having a career in games until fairly late in life," she said. Part of the problem, she added, is the lack of outreach to young girls in middle and high school to let them know there are exciting, rewarding careers in the gaming industry. The article also notes a common but incorrect assumption people make: that women don't play games.

Men and women both enjoy gaming. However, their gaming experiences differ. According to "Video Games: Males Prefer Violence While

Females Prefer Social," a 2012 study released by the Software Usability Research Laboratory at Wichita State University, men are drawn mostly to games of strategy, role playing, action, and fighting. By comparison, women tend to play games from the social, puzzle/card, music/dance, educational/entertainment, and simulation genres. Women also play violent, role-playing games as well. Men treat gaming as a full-fledged hobby while women view gaming as one of several entertainment options.

Despite the growing number of female gamers, women have been the least welcome in Internet

TOP 12 MOST INSPIRATIONAL FEMALE CHARACTERS IN GAMES

Video games still tend to showcase female characters in romantic or damsel-in-distress roles. However, there are a handful of female characters that do more than complement their male counterparts. These twelve female characters were designed to be real, strong, and inspirational main characters.

1. Lara Croft (*Tomb Raider*)
2. Ellie (*The Last of Us*)
3. Major Greenland (*Battlefield 4*)
4. Alyx Vance (*Half-Life 2*)
5. Bayonetta (*Bayonetta*)
6. GlaDos (*Portal 2*)
7. Faith (*Mirror's Edge*)
8. Samus Aran (*Metroid*)
9. Cate Archer (*No One Lives Forever*)
10. Commander Shepard (*Mass Effect*)
11. Haruka (*Yakuza*)
12. Samantha (*Gone Home*)

gaming communities where gamers communicate, play games together, and share information.

WHERE THE GIRLS AREN'T

Anita Sarkeesian knows she offends certain portions of the gaming community. Her opinions about women in gaming—specifically the lack of positive represen-tation of female characters in games and the gender imbalance of female employees in the industry—are not welcome by everyone. Sarkeesian is a media critic and the creator of *Feminist Frequency*, a video Web series that explores representations of women in

Anita Sarkeesian has been the target of harassment and death threats. She has been forced to cancel public appearances to protect both herself and those interested in attending her events.

pop culture. In 2013 and 2014, she launched a video series called *Tropes vs. Women in Video Games*, which analyzed the depiction of women in video games. Some male gamers were enraged. They took to the Internet with crude and inappropriate comments aimed at Sarkeesian. In 2014, after the sixth video in the series was released, Sarkeesian was the target of rape and death threats and was forced to flee her home when her personal information, including her home address, was published online. In an interview with *Wired* magazine, Sarkeesian said, "I knew that delving into video games might provoke a bit of a misogynist backlash … [but] this level of organized and sustained harassment, vitriol, threats of violence and sexual assault…is very telling."

Sarkeesian isn't the only woman to experience harassment by the male-dominated gaming community. In October 2014, the Pew Research Center released its latest findings on online harassment aimed at women between the ages of eighteen and twenty-four:

- 26 percent have been stalked online
- 25 percent were the target of online sexual harassment
- 73 percent say they've witnessed some kind of threats or embarrassment online
- 40 percent have experienced being called offensive names

Harassment is just one part of the problem. Many female gaming professionals feel their male colleagues don't take them seriously. Anna Sweet, who is in business development at Valve and gained experience in the gaming industry as developer and project manager for Microsoft and Myspace, told the

Rochester Institute of Technology's publication, *RIT: The University Magazine*, that while she never felt out of place in the male-dominated gaming industry, she has had some interesting experiences at business meetings. "Someone will inevitably ask a technical question and they will turn to one of my male counterparts. Then those male counterparts will turn back and look at me and then I'll answer the question. Everyone always looks confused when that happens."

The gaming industry is working to counter the attitudes of male gamers, mainly because they don't want to alienate women, who are a significant and growing population of their audience. In addition, male gamers don't all share the same view of female gamers. Many want more inclusion of female characters that present a positive view of women.

Chapter two

CAREERS IN GAMING AND VIDEO GAME DEVELOPMENT

It takes a team of professionals with expertise in a wide range of areas to produce and develop video games. The gaming industry offers many career paths so no matter where your interests lie, there's an option for you.

Behind the creation, design, and development of a video game is a team of professionals who take an idea from conception through its launch as a full-fledged gaming product. The type of game, its complexity, and the depth of its programming needs determine how long it will take a team to produce a game. Simple games can be completed in a few months. Complex, multilevel, multiplayer games can take years to develop before they become available to the public.

FROM CONCEPTION TO COMPLETION: HOW A GAME IS MADE

Creating a game is a collaboration of many people, but it all begins with an idea. Ideas for games may be original, or they may be influenced by popular films, books, comic books, historical events, board games, or television shows. Most ideas begin simple: what

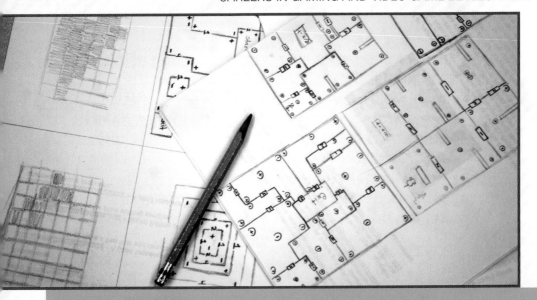

Conceptualizing a video game requires planning every detail—characters, plot, setting, levels, goals of each level, and the purpose of the game—before a designer illustrates a single character or a developer writes the first line of code.

is the game about? Full-fledged details are developed later in one of three phases: pre-production, production, and post-production.

PRE-PRODUCTION

Once an idea is approved for pre-production, a team of producers, designers, programmers, artists, and writers begin to add details to the initial game idea. These details include writing the game's storyline and plot, creating characters and defining what their roles or purposes are, creating storyboards, and putting together a comprehensive document that serves as a blueprint for the game's goals, what happens on each of the game's levels and what those levels will look like, and the gameplay mechanics, such as how players advance through the game and how the game is won or lost. Each of the game's worlds or levels is fully illustrated as well as each individual screen of the game. The details of the document are very specific, down to what happens on a particular screen when the player presses a certain key on a game controller or a particular button on the computer keyboard.

PRODUCTION

After the pre-production blueprint is finalized, the game moves into its production phase, and a larger team is assembled. This team might include a bigger group of producers, programmers, designers, developers, artists, animators, and writers. Each team member has specific responsibilities. Producers make sure the entire team works together to achieve their goals. They manage schedules and deadlines. Designers make sure artists, illustrators, and programmers are implementing the details that were finalized during the pre-production phase. Artists create the animation of the game's world, including environments, buildings, characters, and objects. Programmers code the game's artificial intelligence and special effects. They create the interactions and movements of every single character and object within the game.

POST-PRODUCTION

This final stage of a game's development happens when all of the code and artistry is complete. At this point, the game is fully functional and can be played.

The game is tested by professional gamers with an eye on finding minor bugs or major flaws. Any issues are reported to the development team to be fixed. At this stage, the game is checked to make sure it meets the specifications of the gaming consoles on which it will be played. Each gaming console has functions that are unique to that system.

STILL A BOYS' CLUB?

The gaming industry has had a reputation for being a boys' club. However, women in the industry say that's not a fair assessment of the field. Many say they

At universities throughout the country, organizations, such as Women in Engineering, hold events to encourage young girls in middle school and high school to explore careers in science, technology, engineering, and mathematics.

don't believe it's any harder to get a job in gaming than it is to break into any other technical career field. And with women making up nearly half of all gamers, companies are striving to recruit more women and be inclusive of women's ideas and contributions.

Kate Edwards, executive director of the International Game Developers Association, told Dice.com, a leading news website for technology careers, that the gaming industry is made up of established, big-name companies like Entertainment Arts and Sony Online Entertainment, as well as smaller, independent studios. The larger companies are more in tune to gender balance and women's issues. "Most typically, larger companies that have had some degree of longevity and experience with workforce issues, like gender balance, do a better job at being inclusive in their practices," Edwards said. "I've heard time and time again that one of the biggest issues is the lack of women who seem interested in entering a game development career." She added, "While the industry has some genuine challenges concerning its demographic imbalance, the root issue is that we really need to bolster the availability of STEM programs for girls and young women, and get them interested in games as a career path."

JOB GROWTH HIGH FOR STEM CAREERS

STEM is an acronym for science, technology, engineering, and mathematics. Jobs in these fields are expected to grow significantly over the next five years. According to the U.S. Bureau of Labor Statistics, STEM jobs will grow 17 percent by 2018. That's double the rate of growth compared to non-STEM occupations.

There is a push to recruit more women into STEM careers. While women currently fill close to half of all jobs in the United States, women fill only 25 percent of STEM jobs. According to the U.S. Department of Commerce, women who work in a STEM field make 33 percent more in salary than women employed in non-STEM fields. A study, "Women in STEM: A Gender Gap to Innovation," released by the U.S. Department of Commerce reports that women who earned a college degree in a STEM field are less likely than their male counterparts to be employed in a STEM occupation. Some of the reasons include a lack of female role models and gender stereotyping. Outreach to female middle and high school students, and raising awareness of the exciting and rewarding career paths in STEM, has been important to increasing the number of women in these fields.

BEGIN YOUR GAMING CAREER NOW

Your gaming and video game development career begins in middle school and high school. Many schools offer computer courses in basic program-ming and coding, computer science, or software design. Students interested in technical careers in gaming, including jobs as designers, developers, or programmers, will want to take advanced mathemat-ics courses and as many computer courses as possible. Students interested in the artistic side of gaming will want to complete art courses in illustra-tion, architecture, graphic design, and 3-D design. Students can also gain experience in gaming through

Students can establish a strong foundation for a gaming career while in high school. Look for summer camps, advanced placement courses, technical courses, and electives in gaming, design, computer programming, web development, and interactive multimedia.

a range of summer camp programs that focus on the game design and development field.

SUMMER CAMPS

Some camps include a range of courses taught by professionals in the gaming industry. Some are day camps (you go home every day) while others are sleepaway camps where you could stay for one week or longer with other campers. Gaming camps cover topics such as game design, game programming, game development for mobile devices, 3-D modeling, level design, and game animation.

TOP UNDERGRADUATE SCHOOLS FOR VIDEO GAME DESIGN

The following institutions have robust majors and minors in areas such as game design, game design and development, digital arts and animation, computer science, and new media interactive development.

1. University of Southern California (Los Angeles, CA)
2. University of Utah (Salt Lake City, UT)
3. DigiPen Institute of Technology (Redmond, WA)
4. Drexel University (Philadelphia, PA)
5. Hampshire College (Amherst, MA)
6. Worcester Polytechnic Institute (Worcester, MA)
7. Rochester Institute of Technology (Rochester, NY)
8. The Art Institute of Vancouver (Vancouver, British Columbia / CAN)
9. Massachusetts Institute of Technology (Cambridge, MA)
10. New York University (New York, NY)
11. Shawnee State University (Portsmouth, OH)
12. Michigan State University (East Lansing, MI)
13. Northeastern University (Boston, MA)
14. Oklahoma Christian University (Edmond, OK)
15. Savannah College of Art and Design (Savannah, GA)
16. Champlain College (Burlington, VT)
17. Becker College (Worcester, MA)
18. Rensselaer Polytechnic Institute (Troy, NY)
19. Vancouver Film School (Vancouver, British Columbia / CAN)
20. DePaul University (Chicago, IL)
21. University of California, Santa Cruz (Santa Cruz, CA)
22. New Jersey Institute of Technology (Newark, NJ)
23. North Carolina State University (Raleigh, NC)
24. New England Institute of Technology (East Greenwich, RI)
25. Ferris State University (Grand Rapids, MI)

EXTRACURRICULAR CLUBS AND ACTIVITIES

If your school has a gaming or computing club, take advantage of these opportunities. You'll be able to gain experience working on teams, making decisions together on a project, and learning to collaborate with a range of skill sets, personalities, and experience levels.

CONTESTS AND COMPETITIONS

These provide a chance for you to compete with others who have an interest and aptitude for gaming. Contests challenge you to design and develop a working game and submit it to a panel of judges who play the game and assess its gameplay mechanics, design, programming, and execution.

Chapter three

DESIGNERS

R obin Hunicke has worked for major gaming companies, including Electronic Arts and thatgamecompany, where she served as a game designer and producer. In an interview with *Hairpin*, she said, "I think that a designer or producer's number one job is to think about the player experience. When listening to a feature proposal or creating

Robin Hunicke speaks at the launch of Marvell's AVANTA broadband product in 2010. Her focus as a game creator is on the user experience.

one, it's important to ask 'What would the player feel?' and, 'Is that what we want?'" She continued, "If your beautiful design creates feelings of frustration or intimidation in players, then what's the use? No one will play your game. A good creative leader asks, 'Does this make the player feel X' where X is a desirable outcome like: smart, creative, masterful."

A CAREER AS A GAME DESIGNER

Game designers are responsible for proposing an initial idea for a game, and once approved for production, they begin planning and developing. Designers create and define all the elements and components of a game, from its setting, environments, structure, rules, storyline, and story flow to its characters, the objects (weapons, vehicles, objects, and other game props) used by characters, and the devices, options, and decisions available for the characters to make as they navigate the game. Game designers need a solid understanding of the different hardware platforms (e.g., personal computer, gaming consoles, mobile devices) a game can be played on and which is best for the type of game they are producing. For example, in a game such as Zynga's *Castleville Legends*, where players build and expand a medieval kingdom, players need to see their kingdom in its entirety in order to send characters on quests and move them through the game. A smartphone, which has a limited screen size, may not be the ideal setting for this game. Designers must identify which device provides the best experience for the player. Designers must also have knowledge of the various software technologies and techniques that work best on each platform.

A game designer is also responsible for making sure the entire gaming team understands the vision and concept of the game. As they work together on crafting the game and its gameplay mechanics, the team must always be on the same page so the designer's vision of the game can be realized.

WORK ENVIRONMENT

Whether they work for large corporate gaming companies or small independent firms, game designers always work on a team. The ability to work collaboratively

To create a game, designers, developers, writers, illustrators, and producers as well as business management professionals, financial personnel, and marketing executives work together.

and with a wide range of other people is necessary for success in the field.

Game designers spend much of their day working on computers. They often have access to the latest software and cutting-edge graphics programs. They also work with a range of other technical hardware to create impressive artwork and realistic sounds for the game.

The work hours can be long for a game designer, especially if the production of a game is nearing a critical deadline.

EDUCATION, TRAINING, AND SKILLS

Game designers must have a solid knowledge of computer systems and understand software and how it works. It's also necessary for game designers to have a background in computer programming, to know multiple programming languages, and to understand the foundations of good game design. Advanced knowledge of computer systems (how computers work individually and as part of a network) is helpful.

A bachelor's degree is the most common educational requirement for entry into the field, though some entry-level positions can be obtained with a two-year associate's degree or a certificate, plus experience gained through internships or cooperative education experiences. Game designers can select from a wide range of degree programs in majors such as game and simulation programming, game design and development, game art, digital entertainment, and new media interactive development. Some game designers major in computer science and complete minors in an area of game design or development.

TOP 20 GAMING COMPANIES

These companies have produced games that have influenced a generation of designers and developers, changed the industry with inventive creations or legendary games, or created new methods of gameplay.

1. Nintendo EAD
(Entertainment and Analysis Division)
2. Capcom
3. Rockstar North
4. Konami
5. Atari
6. SquareSoft
7. Valve
8. Blizzard Entertainment
9. EA Maxis
10. id Software
11. LucasArts
12. Looking Glass Studios
13. Bethesda Game Studios
14. BioWare
15. HAL Laboratory
16. Naughty Dog
17. Ubisoft Montreal
18. Enix
19. MicroProse Software
20. Insomniac Games

Degree programs cover coursework in topics such as visual design, modeling, programming languages, game design, interactive media development, game studies, 2-D and 3-D animation, Web design and implementation, interface design, multiplayer gaming environments, usability testing, designing games for mobile devices, and gaming business and management.

Some advanced game design positions, such as lead designer or game design manager, call for a master's degree. A master's degree is an advanced degree beyond a four-year bachelor's degree. It allows students to specialize in a particular area. Many game designers move up the ranks of a gaming company to become project leaders or production managers. These positions benefit from advanced knowledge of management, marketing, finance, and other operational knowledge that comes from a master's degree in business, finance, or management. Some master's degrees in game design and development include advanced courses in business and management.

Internships and cooperative education experiences give those interested in gaming careers a chance to complete real assignments and be a part of an actual gaming team.

INTERNSHIPS, CO-OPS, WORK EXPERIENCES

Internships and cooperative education experiences (co-ops) will provide you with hands-on experience working for a gaming company. You may work under the supervision of a game designer where you may be responsible for creating one or two aspects of a game. Internships and co-ops give you firsthand knowledge of what it is like to work in the gaming industry and how a collaborative gaming team works together to produce a finished product. These experiences look great on your résumé and you can make contacts in the field that can be helpful for when you are ready to apply for your first professional employment position.

Chapter four

DEVELOPERS

Erin Robinson has been making games as a hobby since she was eighteen years old. She began interacting with an online community of adventure game developers where she found an encouraging group of fellow developers. She never considered game development as a career until she was approached by Wadjet Eye Games to develop artwork for a game called *Puzzle Bots*. When the project led to a full-time developer position, she jumped at the chance to work full-time in the games industry. She has been instrumental in developing games for Wadjet Eye Games, including *Spooks* and *Nanobots*.

BECOMING A GAME DEVELOPER

Game developers, also called software developers, have an important role in the production of a game. They turn the ideas of the designers, producers, graphic artists, and writers into code. Programming languages such as C++, JavaScript, Python, HTML, and CSS provide the computer or gaming console with the game's operating instructions. Writing programming code is the main function of a game developer. Developers use programming code to bring to life the various elements of the games, from the game's story, characters, and role-play mechanics to animation and the game environment.

Game developers are also heavily involved in testing and debugging the game's software and maintaining and improving it once the game is operational and available to consumers. Occasionally, games have new versions and an upgrade is available to players. These upgrades can include new characters or advanced levels of play, or they may fix bugs and problems discovered in early versions. Game developers are the ones who create the upgrades.

The day-to-day work of a developer can include:

- Writing detailed design documentation, including charts and diagrams that outline the various concepts and components involved in the development of a game
- Writing and modifying code for a game
- Rewriting code to solve a problem
- Training game testers
- Preparing digital graphics, animation, video, sound, photos, and other multimedia assets for production

WORK ENVIRONMENT

Depending on the size of the production team and the type of game being produced, developers may work with several other developers where each is responsible for a different aspect of the game. On smaller projects, a developer might code the entire game by herself. Being able to work collaboratively with game designers, producers, animators, writers, and sound engineers is also necessary.

These lines of programming code tell a computer to perform certain tasks. Game developers learn the language of programming to create different elements of gameplay.

Like all members of the production team, some days may require long hours, especially if an important production deadline is approaching.

EDUCATION, TRAINING, AND SKILLS

Game developers have several educational options available, from certificate programs to two- and four-year degree options. Most important to the game developer's job is programming skill. You should seek out programs that place an emphasis on learning programming languages. Languages such as C++,

JavaScript, OOP, Assembly, C#, Smalltalk, Eiffel, Lua, and Python are used regularly to program various aspects of a video game. Proficiency in these languages is necessary for success as a game developer.

Additional skills needed include an understanding of animation, basic design skills, competency in story and plot development, and communication skills. Developers need to present their portions of a gaming project and be able to talk through the development process in terms that non-developers can understand.

TOP PROGRAMMING LANGUAGES FOR GAME DEVELOPMENT

Programming languages are designed to communicate instructions to a machine. Game developers use many different types of programming languages, but these in particular are among the most popular and widely used.

- C++: This is the most popular game-development language. It is used to develop software systems, application software, and video games, and covers the full spectrum of gaming platforms.
- Java: Java is an industry standard used in game development, for mobile apps, and for web-based content.
- HTML5, CSS, PHP, and JavaScript: All four of these programming languages are used exclusively for browser and mobile-based game development.

INTERNSHIPS AND CO-OPS

Some of the larger companies, such as Blizzard Entertainment, have internship programs where they actively seek out interns and co-ops each year to work on various projects. Most companies are seeking interns who are enrolled in a bachelor's or master's degree program in game design and development, computer science, mathematics, programming, or a related field. Candidates also need to have demonstrated programming experience and have a strong knowledge of programming languages. Companies don't want to train you on programming languages. Instead, they want you to be

A knowledge of some programming language is important for any aspect of game designing.

knowledgeable enough to be given portions of a project to work on independently under the supervision of an experienced developer or producer. Companies also look for interns who have basic knowledge of areas such as artificial intelligence, gameplay logic, pathing, various operating systems, user interface, scripting, and animation tools.

Internships are a great way to learn in a hands-on environment, be part of a team that is actively producing a video game, and gain valuable experience you can add to your résumé when it's time to search for a full-time position.

Each company decides how they choose to compensate their interns. Internships may be paid positions, or students may get college credit.

Chapter five

PROGRAMMERS

A video game programmer is a software engineer who creates the code that makes a video game run. Video game programmers are responsible for implementing the vision of the game designer and making sure the game runs smoothly and without problems. Once the game

Before a game is final, programmers need to code how a character will move and interact with every possible game element.

designer and the game developer finalize the vision of the game, its environment, and how it will be played, the game programmer steps in to begin coding.

The game programmer develops computer code to determine the speed of a moving object, how a character moves or uses a gameplay object such as a tool or weapon, and how the character interacts with its environment. Coding must be accurate. For example, a human character's hands must accurately represent actual hands and their movement, including gestures, and must be true to how human hands move in real life.

It is also the game programmer's responsibility to ensure the game doesn't crash during gameplay and that the game runs smoothly through the duration of the game. The more complex or complicated a game is, the more challenging the programmer's task is to write code that makes the game operate smoothly.

TYPES OF PROGRAMMERS

With such a wide range of games on the market, from simple puzzle games to complex, multiplayer games that mimic real life, it's difficult to be proficient in all areas of game programming. As a result, most programmers specialize in one or two areas of programming.

NETWORK PROGRAMMER

Playing with or against other players in your living room or across the country is a dynamic aspect to modern gaming made possible by the Internet. A network programmer's job is to make sure games operate correctly on the Internet. This requires not only a programming background but also knowledge of WAN (wide area network) and the ability to write code that allows multiple players to play together despite being separated geographically.

VIDEO GAME TESTER

All the different pieces of a game—every character and prop, each screen, and all of the game's various levels—must be tested to see how a player might potentially break the game or find a loophole. It's the game tester's job to play a game and execute every potential action or decision of a character on every level to find a problem. Testers are often game programmers or developers who are experts in gameplay. They spend hours each day playing games and are experienced in finding all the various ways to break a game or execute an action that can instantly win a game or bring it to an end.

Game testers report their gaming experience back to the programmers and developers so problems and other issues can be fixed before the game is released publicly. Game testers need an educational background in game programming, game development, computer science, or a related computing field. They must be able to communicate effectively in order to express their concerns about a game to the production team. Game testers can work for a gaming company or may be hired only when a game is ready for testing. Once the testing is completed, testers move on to other projects.

ARTIFICIAL INTELLIGENCE PROGRAMMER

AI technology enables realistic, intelligent behavior to occur in gaming characters. In many games, there are computer-controlled players who work with you or may be your enemy. There is no person choosing the behavior of these characters. AI programmers create these characters and the computer is programmed to choose how these characters behave based on the choices of other players in the game.

USER INTERFACE PROGRAMMER

User interface is how a player interacts with a game. A user interface programmer makes sure that players can easily control everything they need to in a game. Is it simple to move a character around? Can you

How a player interacts with a game is part of the user experience. Here, two gamers play with *Dance Central 2*, on the Kinect system.

collect items with a click of a button? User interface programmers think about players and their interaction with the game.

WORK ENVIRONMENT

Game programmers must have a solid knowledge of gaming console systems. Programmers code games based on the gaming system used to play the game. PlayStation, GameBoy, and Xbox all have different system requirements that require a programmer to be familiar with each and program accordingly. Like other positions on a game production team, being able to work on a team and collaborate with others is essential, especially if you are programming only one

Designers need to be aware of industry platforms. This Sony PSP handheld device will be different from the handheld device of another gaming company.

aspect of the game. You must be working and communicating regularly with your team to ensure that everyone has the same goals and objectives in mind.

EDUCATION REQUIREMENTS

Due to the advanced knowledge of programming and coding needed by these positions, programmers must have a bachelor's or master's degree in computer science, game programming, mathematics, or a related field. These academic programs provide instruction in courses such as programming languages, computing coding, computer systems, software engineering, data management, data structures, computer organization, advanced mathematics, and design and analysis of efficient algorithms. Programming majors are highly math intensive, so strong math skills are a must for success in both an academic program and in a professional position.

Chapter six

ANIMATORS, AUDIO ENGINEERS, AND WRITERS

I n addition to game designers, developers, and programmers, video games need artwork, sound, and a storyline to add to the gaming experience. Animators, audio engineers, and writers provide invaluable contributions to the gaming team.

ANIMATORS AND ARTISTS

Lionel Gallat was an established animator in the film industry, where he worked on films such as *The Prince of Egypt, The Road to Eldorado, SharkTale,* and *Flushed Away*. He decided to move into video game animation to take advantage of a faster production process. "Movie development moves at a much slower pace. Iterations can take hours, sometimes days," he told Gamasutra, an online news site for the gaming industry. "So in my experience this change of pipeline translates into more freedom in the workflow."

Gallat's first animated gaming project is *Ghost of a Tale*, a game with movielike animations. He told Gamasutra that his movie animation skills mirror

Animators draw both characters and scenery for a game using computer design software. Games often have an animation style that they need to learn so that the images are consistent.

those needed in gaming and the only major difference is the attention to detail one must give to films. "I would say one big difference between movies and games is that on a movie we tend to nitpick about many things. The attention to detail is pushed to excruciating lengths. It's mostly due to the screen size movies are projected on, and the complex simulation calculations going on at render time. With games you can be a lot more loose in your approach. It's much more forgiving and I really like that."

Gallat, like all game animators, creates the 2-D and 3-D visible elements of a game. Animators decide how everything in a game will look, including characters, the environment of the game, objects and settings, and even the lighting. They create the movement of characters, down to their clothing and their facial expressions, as well as objects in the gaming environment, like flowing water.

Video game animators can have a range of jobs depending on the size of the game and the production team. On smaller games, an animator might do nearly all of the artwork themselves. On larger projects, an animator might be responsible for one or two components of the animation. These jobs include texture artist, character artist, environment or world artist, or effects artist. Animators may specialize in a singular area of animation.

To become a video game animator or artist, a certificate program and two-year degree in fine arts or animation will provide you with a foundation in fine art. Basic fine art courses will cover subjects such as art theory, art history, composition, color, form, space, and light. Bachelor's degrees in programs such as illustration, animation, or graphic design will include the coursework you need to fine-tune your art skills. These programs include courses that cover topics such as the principles of animation, animation techniques, 2-D and 3-D drawing, animation scripting and storyboarding, visual effects, computer graphics, digital animation, animation production, and character design. Many bachelor's degree programs offer minors where you can learn an additional set of skills beyond your degree program. Minors are a set of four to six courses in a particular area of study. Animators who want to work in the games industry might want to complete a minor in game design, 3-D computer animation, or experimental animation.

AUDIO ENGINEERS

Adding sound effects to a game is the responsibility of the audio engineer. Sound effects can include music, voices, spoken instructions, and ambient sounds such as gunfire, rain, tires squealing, crowd noise, or animal sounds. Audio engineers are responsible for finding or creating sound effects and editing, mixing, and mastering the music and sounds to produce the soundtrack for the finished game.

Whether its background music or gunshots, sound is an important part of gameplay. Audio engineers are responsible for making sure sounds are realistic and accurate in the world of a game.

Many audio and sound professionals are self-taught or learn their skills by completing internships and co-ops. For those interested in completing formal coursework, certificate programs and two- and four-year degrees in audio engineering provide instruction in acoustics and psychoacoustics, computer music composition and arrangement, sound recording, sound production, multitrack recording, critical listening, digital sound synthesis, and media arts. Many programs also include classes in electrical engineering, digital signal processing, and music technology. Many audio and sound professionals are trained musicians.

Audio jobs in the gaming industry are highly competitive. Game development teams don't always have their own audio engineer. It's common practice for one audio or sound engineer to work on multiple production teams. Many are also contract positions, which means they don't work directly for the company producing the game but instead are hired per job. When the work is completed, they move on to other projects, even other companies.

WRITERS

A writer creates a game's storyline, its characters' stories, the game's plot, and its narrative. Writers help video game designers craft an immersive, interactive narrative experience for players. A game should start someplace interesting, progress through an interactive, engaging storyline, and conclude in a satisfying manner. While gameplay must be the main priority, a game's plot can make the difference between an engaging storyline versus a flat narrative that makes the game boring to play.

A video game writer becomes involved in a game from the pre-production stage. The writer can help the game designer work through the initial idea, as well as develop basic storylines and characters that will be developed more fully in the later stages of production. Writers can create a detailed outline of the game's story, plot, and setting, including a description of individual scenes and gameplay objectives,

Storyboards are visual tools used by writers to help them craft the story behind a game. Storyboards can help a writer determine plot points, develop characters, and keep the story interesting for the gamer.

such as finding a jewel, stealing a car, assassinating a government official, or taming a dragon.

Writers often complete coursework in English, creative writing, or journalism, where they sharpen their writing skills with courses in composition, storytelling, and narrative design. Additional courses might include character development, establishing a plot, and story pacing and movement.

Many video game writers start out as fans who write about their favorite games or about the gaming industry. This is how Jessica Chobot got her start writing games. Chobot stated as an on-air host for

IGN, an online media and services company with a focus on gaming, presenting at events around the world and reviewing video games. She was asked to draft an outline for a horror game and the result was *Daylight*.

Daylight is the first of its kind and a game changer for the video games industry in terms of scripting and plot. The game is procedurally generated, meaning each time you play the game it will be different. Currently games have one storyline and once you master the game, playing it again provides the same experience. *Daylight* is challenging that norm.

Chapter seven

LANDING YOUR FIRST GAMING JOB

You've studied hard and gotten experience at a gaming company through an internship or co-op, and now you're ready to begin applying for your first professional position in the gaming industry. With a projected growth of 17 percent by 2018, job opportunities are available for those with the skills and knowledge to design and develop the next generation of games. Your job search strategy begins with creating a résumé, drafting a cover letter, identifying positions you are qualified for, and acing the interview.

CREATE AN EYE-CATCHING RÉSUMÉ

Your job search begins with a well-written, well-organized, and nicely designed résumé. It is important to make a good first impression because this is the first thing a hiring manager sees. A résumé will tell a potential employer all about the work experience you gained while on co-ops or through internships; any education you completed, including coursework and special projects you were a part of; the computer skills you have

The annual Electronic Entertainment Expo, or E3, is a popular spot for emerging game designers, developers, programmers, and others to network with gaming professionals for jobs and internships.

mastered; projects you participated in, such as games you had a role in designing or developing; and any special abilities, awards, or recognition you've earned.

Hiring managers receive a lot of résumés so yours must stand out. A résumé that is hastily created, disorganized, or otherwise unpleasant to look at tells a hiring manager that you haven't invested the time in preparing your résumé. No matter how accomplished you are, a well thought-out résumé that is easy to read is essential. Your résumé should be organized into multiple sections, with each one focused on a particular set of credentials, such as education, experience, skills, awards, etc. Each of these sections should be organized in chronological order, with the most recent listing first. Many vocational schools, community colleges, and four-year colleges and universities have professionals skilled in creating résumés. Their expertise can be invaluable to you if you are creating your very first professional résumé. These professionals can be found in your school's career services office.

YOUR PORTFOLIO: HIGHLIGHTING THE BEST YOU HAVE TO OFFER

Some jobs in the gaming industry, such as those in animation, graphic design, Web design and development, or illustration, may require you to submit a portfolio. A

Your portfolio is a representation of your work. It's the place where you can show off your web design, animation, illustration, writing, and graphic design skills.

professional portfolio shows off your creative abilities through projects you've completed for class assignments, during internships or co-ops, or via independent work. Most portfolios are presented via a website and should contain the following:

A SHORT ARTIST'S STATEMENT OR BIOGRAPHY

An artist's statement is a brief description of your work that provides some context of the work or introduces the work in the portfolio. The statement can also include biographical information, such as your career aspirations, education, and any awards you've won for your creative work.

SAMPLES OF YOUR BEST WORK

Your portfolio is a presentation of your best work, so it should include only completed projects that represent your finest illustrations, graphic designs, and multimedia animations. Your portfolio should contain high-quality images of artwork or illustrations, links to the live versions of websites you've designed, live links to any online gaming or multimedia animation you've created, or samples of projects you've completed as part of high school or college classes. Most artists have both an online portfolio and a physical one for meetings.

CONDUCTING AN ONLINE JOB SEARCH

It's exciting to search for a job. It's a time full of potential and promise as you decide what types of positions in gaming you are interested in pursuing. Searching the Internet for a job can seem overwhelming, but knowing how and where to look to find the best positions will help you save time and identify open positions faster.

VISIT COMPANY WEBSITES

Spend time searching the websites of gaming companies you would like to work for. Each company posts available jobs, and some provide inside knowledge on how to apply for jobs and what it's like to work for their company.

SEARCH YOUR NICHE

Conduct a search of gaming industry job websites. These sites are full of open positions at all types of gaming companies and provide one place to search for a large number of jobs.

POST YOUR RÉSUMÉ

Use industry websites or the job boards of professional video gaming organizations to post your résumé. Hiring managers and recruiters often search these sites to identify candidates that meet the initial requirements for open positions.

CREATE A CANDIDATE PROFILE

Many company websites feature career pages where you can complete a personal profile that lists your

GAMING INDUSTRY JOB SEARCH WEBSITES

A number of websites list vacancies at major gaming companies as well as at smaller independent studios. Some sites require you to become a member by paying a small initial membership fee. Membership often comes with added benefits such as being able to post your résumé to the site for recruiters and being able to contact companies directly with questions about open jobs. Some sites also list international positions.

job interests and aspirations, educational credentials, and work experiences. When a position opens that matches your profile, the company may reach out to you directly.

BUILD A PROFESSIONAL NETWORK

You may have heard the phrase "It's who you know." Networking is a business term for connecting to professionals working in your career field or in related career fields. These professionals can help mentor you as you begin building your gaming career, provide guidance on work issues such as asking for a raise or seeking a promotion, and offer general support. Many times when companies have open positions, managers look to their own professional contacts for suggestions.

PREPARING FOR AN INTERVIEW

Your résumé highlights your abilities, education, and experience in the field, but it doesn't tell a hiring manager if you have the right personality for that company, if you'll fit in well with the staff, or if you'll excel in a particular work environment. This is the purpose of an interview.

An interview is an opportunity for you to talk directly with the people you'll potentially be working with. It's a chance for a company to learn about you and for you to learn about a company. In an interview, you should focus on learning more in-depth information about the job you're applying for, and you should assess if this is the type of company or people you want to work with. In an interview, you should always act professionally. Turn off your cell phone, leave gum and mints at home, avoid bringing food or drinks with you, and make sure to dress professionally. Plan to arrive early, especially if the location of the office is unfamiliar or if you antici-pate traffic. If possible, drive to the location a few days before your appointment to map out where you'll park and how to get into the building. Some large compa-nies can have multiple locations. You don't want to be rushing into an interview or feel flustered or nervous because you got lost.

YOUR FIRST JOB

Congratulations, you've been hired! Your first job is always exciting. The culmination of all your hard work has paid off. But now is not the time to rest.

Your first professional gaming job is a chance for you to soak up as much information as possible.

TIPS FOR A SUCCESSFUL INTERVIEW

- **Plan ahead:** Research the company you are interviewing with. What does it do? What products does it make? Who are its competitors? Prepare some questions that show you know about the company and are interested in finding out more.

- **Play games created by the company:** Your interviewer might ask what you like about the company's games or what ideas you have for improving them.

- **Make eye contact:** This shows your interest in the job and in the person you're speaking with.

- **Be positive:** Don't speak negatively about past employers.

- **Listen:** Be aware of what the interviewer is saying about his or her company and the job you are interviewing for. Ask follow-up questions to show you are engaged in the conversation, listening to what is being said, and interested in the company and the job.

- **Focus on your achievements:** When answering questions, demonstrate what you know and how you would adapt your knowledge to particular gaming projects.

There will be ample opportunities to learn—from new projects to experienced, talented colleagues. While working at your first job, remember the following tips.

Your first job is just that, the first in a long line of professional opportunities that await you. Your first job is a stepping-stone that can lead to promotions, new jobs at different companies, and possibly a new career field.

Take time to learn the ropes of your new workplace. Two of the biggest complaints companies have about first-time employees is that they often expect to be assigned more responsibility than they are prepared for and they tend to think they know more than seasoned employees. One of the best things you can do is listen. Listen to your supervisors, pay attention to the veteran employees, and take in as much information as you can.

Learn how decisions are made, who has the final say and who has the most influence on decisions so that you know who to go to if you have an idea.

Each company has its own culture. Look at how employees behave, dress, and discuss work to learn the unwritten rules of etiquette.

Ask for feedback often. If you want to know what you are doing well or areas where you can improve, ask your supervisor. Seek out opportunities to improve your performance and learn new things. You should also know what is expected of you. Having an open dialogue with your supervisor can eliminate confusion later about assigned tasks and responsibilities.

Chapter eight

A LIFELONG CAREER IN GAMING

Anna Sweet began her career in gaming with an internship at Microsoft Games Studio, where she worked with the Xbox group. The internship led to a full-time position in Microsoft's shared technology group after she graduated with a degree in computer science from Rochester Institute of Technology. After a few years, Sweet decided she didn't want to code all day long, so she accepted a position at Myspace in project management, where she led forty project managers in offices in Seattle, Los Angeles, and San Francisco. Sweet liked working with people, but she missed the games industry, so she moved on to Valve to work on Steam, the company's game platform.

Sweet's movement through the gaming and computing industry, where she learned new skills and gained management experience with each new position, is a natural part of advancing in the games industry. Moving up and moving around is one way to gain experience and excel. Another way is to earn an advanced degree.

An advanced degree can help you earn higher levels of responsibility in the games industry. You'll gain an expertise in a particular area of gaming, where you can excel and become a leader in the field.

ADVANCED DEGREES IN GAMING

An advanced degree in gaming, game development and design, interactive media, or entertainment arts and engineering is a one- to two-year program that provides a focus on the development, production, and design of video games. Unlike certificate programs or two- and four-year degree programs, which establish a solid foundation of knowledge in a particular area of gaming, an advanced degree emphasizes the skills, knowledge, and techniques needed for particular roles in the games industry.

TOP 10 GRADUATE SCHOOLS FOR GAME DESIGN AND DEVELOPMENT

These schools offer master of science degrees in various areas of gaming that provide an in-depth study of game design and development. These programs provide advanced coursework in game play and prototyping, advanced processes for game development, game industry themes and perspectives, interactivity, 3-D modeling, advanced animation, and digital media. You'll need a bachelor's degree in a related career field, such as game design, game development, computer science, or new media interactive design to be considered for enrollment.

1. University of Southern California (Los Angeles, CA)
2. University of Central Florida (Orlando, FL)
3. Southern Methodist University (Dallas, TX)
4. University of Utah (Salt Lake City, UT)
5. DigiPen Institute of Technology (Redmond, WA)
6. Drexel University (Philadelphia, PA)
7. University of California, Santa Cruz (Santa Cruz, CA)
8. Rochester Institute of Technology (Rochester, NY)
9. New York University (New York, NY)
10. Massachusetts Institute of Technology (Cambridge, MA)

Graduate degrees can lead to promotions, higher salaries, and better opportunities for advancement. Those with master's degrees may be preferred to those without when applying to jobs. Those with graduate degrees have advanced knowledge, skills, and training, which can lead to being better prepared to take on more complex projects at work.

FOLLOW ADVANCEMENTS IN YOUR FIELD

Gaming is technology-based, and with all technology, something new is always on the horizon. Fifteen years ago the gaming industry was confined to PCs and home gaming consoles. Tablets and smartphones opened up a new audience for gaming companies and drew more people to embrace different kinds of games, such as *Angry Birds* and *Candy Crush*, which can be played on phones and tablets. These games don't require the time

The latest trend in gaming is mobile devices. There will be more opportunities than ever before to create games the user can play via a smartphone or other mobile device.

commitment or monthly financial investment of a multiplayer, intensive experience like *World of Warcraft* or *Assassin's Creed.*

Staying aware of the latest advancements in technology and how they might influence the gaming industry can help you advance your career. There will always be new technology or a new way to use existing software. New research will continue to inform game designers and developers on how to better create the gaming experience for the player. Staying on top of these trends can help you evolve in the industry as well.

ATTEND INDUSTRY CONFERENCES AND EVENTS

E3, the Electronic Entertainment Expo, is one of the largest annual trade conventions and expos in the gaming industry. It's a chance for gaming insiders to come together to learn about the latest product launches and groundbreaking technologies used in gaming today, and hear major news announcements about the industry. It's also the place to be to network with industry experts and see the latest trends in gaming before they are available to the public.

JOIN A PROFESSIONAL GAMING ORGANIZATION

E3 is just one of many industry events and conferences you can attend. To learn more about these opportunities, join a professional gaming organization, such as the Entertainment Software Association or the American Gaming Association. These organizations organize regional, state, or national conferences; produce a newsletter or magazine on industry news and trends; and offer networking, job searches, and professional development opportunities. You can meet other gaming professionals and learn about the latest technologies and trends that affect the gaming industry.

Glossary

ACOUSTICS A science that deals with the production, control, transmission, reception, and effects of sound.

AMBIENT SOUND Background noise.

ARTIFICIAL INTELLIGENCE An area of computer science that deals with giving machines the ability to seem like they have human intelligence.

BLUEPRINT A detailed plan of how to do something.

CODE Instructions for a computer.

FRANCHISE The right or license granted to an individual or group to market a company's goods or services in a particular territory.

GAME CONSOLE A device that uses a visual interactive display that can be used to play video games.

GAMEPLAY MECHANICS The combination and interaction of many elements of a game.

ITERATIONS Repeating blocks of statements within a computer program with the goal of getting closer to a desired outcome.

NICHE A job or activity suited to a particular person.

PATHING An approach to networking that attempts to assess the best way to meet a network's storage needs.

PLATFORM The computer architecture and equipment using a particular operating system.

PSYCHOACOUSTICS A branch of science dealing with the perception of sound, the sensations produced by sounds, and the problems of communication.

RENDER To use a computer program to create an image from one or more models.

SIMULATION The imitation of real-world situations.

STEREOTYPING Believing unfairly that all people or things with a particular characteristic are the same.

STORYBOARD A series of drawings or pictures that show the changes of scenes and actions for a movie, television show, video game, etc.

WAN (WIDE AREA NETWORK) Any network that covers a large area, which can be across towns or spanning several countries.

For More Information

Digital Games Research Association (DiGRA)
E-mail: coordinator@digra.org
Website: http://www.digra.org/
DiGRA is for academics and professionals who
    research digital games and associated phe-
    nomena. It encourages high-quality research on
    games and promotes collaboration and dissemi-
    nation of work by its members.

Entertainment Software Association of Canada (ESA)
130 Spadina Avenue, Suite 408
Toronto, ON M5V 2L4
Canada
(416) 620-7171
Website: http://theesa.ca
The ESA of Canada is the voice of the Canadian
    computer and video game industry, which employs
    approximately 16,500 people at over 325 compa-
    nies across the country.

Interactive Ontario (IO)
431 King Street West
Suite 600
Toronto, ON M5V 1K4
Canada
(416) 516-0077
Website: http://www.interactiveontario.com
Interactive Ontario is a not-for-profit industry trade
    organization committed to the growth of the
    Ontario interactive digital content industry.

International Game Developers Association
19 Mantua Road

Mt. Royal, NJ 08061
(856) 423-2990
Website: http://www.igda.org
The IGDA is a global network of collaborative proj-
    ects and communities comprised of individuals
    from all fields of game development—from pro-
    grammers and producers to writers, artists, QA,
    and localization. Its mission is to advance the
    careers and enhance the lives of game developers
    by connecting members with their peers, promot-
    ing professional development, and advocating for
    issues that affect the developer community.

Women in Games International
E-mail: info@getwigi.com
Website: http://www.womeningamesinternational.org
Women in Games International advocates for issues
    important to the success of all genders in the
    games industry and works to promote the inclu-
    sion and advancement of women in the global
    games industry.

WEBSITES

Because of the changing nature of Internet links,
Rosen Publishing has developed an online list of
websites related to the subject of this book. This site
is updated regularly. Please use this link to access
the list:

http://www.rosenlinks.com/TECH/Game

For Further Reading

Brathwaite, Brenda, and Ian Schreiber. *Challenges for Game Designers: Non-Digital Exercises for Video Game Designers.* Independence, KY: Cengage Learning, 2008.

Briggs, Jason R. *Python for Kids: A Playful Introduction to Programming.* San Francisco, CA: No Starch Press, 2012.

Dille, Flint, and John Zuur Platten. *The Ultimate Guide to Video Game Writing and Design.* Los Angeles, CA: Lone Eagle Publishing, 2008.

Dunniway, Troy, and Jeannie Novak. *Game Development Essentials: Gameplay Mechanics.* Independence, KY: Cengage Learning, 2008.

Funk, Joe. *Cool Careers in Interactive Development: Hot Jobs in Video Games.* New York, NY: Scholastic, 2010.

Kaplan, Arie. *The Crazy Careers of Video Game Designers.* Minneapolis, MN: Lerner Publishing Group, 2013.

Kennedy, Sam R. *How to Become a Video Game Artist: The Insider's Guide to Landing a Job in the Gaming World.* New York, NY: Crown Publishing Group/Watson-Guptill, 2013.

Knight, Gladys L. *Female Action Heroes: A Guide to Women in Comics, Video Games, Film and Television.* Westport, CT: Greenwood Press, 2010.

Lengyel, Eric. *Mathematics for 3D Game Programming and Computer Graphics.* Independence, KY: Cengage Learning, 2011.

McShaffry, Mike, and David Graham. *Game Coding Complete.* Independence, KY: Cengage Learning, 2012.

Novak, Jeannie, and Travis Castillo. *Game Development Essentials: Game Level Design.* Independence, KY: Cengage Learning, 2008.

Rogers, Scott. *Level Up! The Guide to Great Video Game Design.* Hoboken, NJ: Wiley Publishers, 2014.

Sande, Warren, and Carter Sande. *Hello World! Computer Programming for Kids and Other Beginners.* Shelter Island, NY: Manning Publications, 2009.

Saunders, Kevin, and Jeannie Novak. *Game Development Essentials: Game Interface Design.* Independence, KY: Cengage Learning, 2012.

Solarski, Chris. *Drawing Basics and Video Game Art: Classic to Cutting-Edge Art Techniques for Winning Video Game Design.* New York, NY: Crown Publishing Group/Watson-Guptill, 2012.

Strom, Chris. *3D Game Programming for Kids: Create Interactive Worlds with JavaScript.* Raleigh, NC: Pragmatic Programmers, 2013.

Sweigart, Al. *Invent Your Own Computer Games with Python.* Sebastopol, CA: O'Reilly Media/Albert\Sweigart, 2010.

Valente, Catherynne, Seanan McGuire, and Racheline Maltese. *Chicks Dig Gaming: A Celebration of All Things Gaming by the Women Who Love It.* Des Moines, IA: Mad Norwegian Press, 2014.

Bibliography

Beede, David, Tiffany Julian, David Langdon, George McKittrick, Beethika Khan, and Mark Doms. "Women in STEM: A Gender Gap to Innovation." August 2011. Retrieved October 30, 2014 (www .esa.doc.gov/sites/default/files/reports/documents /womeninstemagaptoinnovation8311.pdf).

Bell, Erin. "Erin Robinson Talks Puzzle Bots." December 2, 2009. Retrieved November 7, 2014 (http:// www.gamezebo.com/2009/12/02/erin-robinson -talks-puzzle-bots).

Culp, Jennifer. "Women and Video Games: Robin Hunicke." August 3, 2012. Retrieved November 11, 2014 (http://thehairpin.com/2012/08/women-and -video-games-robin-hunicke).

Duggan, Maeve. "Online Harassment: Summary of Findings." October 22, 2014. Retrieved October 30, 2014 (http://www.pewinternet.org/2014/10/22/ online-harassment).

Entertainment Software Association. "2014 Essential Facts." Retrieved October 31, 2014 (http://www .theesa.com/facts/index.asp).

Frank, Jenn. "How to Attack a Woman Who Works in Gaming." September 1, 2014. Retrieved October 30, 2014 (http://www.theguardian.com/technology /2014/sep/01/how-to-attack-a-woman-who-works -in-video-games).

Game Design Schools. "Advancing Your Game Design Career." Retrieved November 12, 2014 (http://game-designschools.com/advancing-your -game-design-career).

Hiscott, Rebecca. "10 Programming Languages You Should Learn Right Now." January 21, 2014.

Retrieved November 12, 2014 (http://mashable
.com/2014/01/21/learn-programming-languages).

Hu, Elise. "Pew: Gaming Is Least Welcoming Online
Space for Women." October 22, 2014. Retrieved
October 30, 2014 (http://www.npr.org/blogs/
alltechconsidered/2014/10/22/357826882/
pew-gaming-is-least-welcoming-online-space
-for-women).

IGN Entertainment. "Top 50 Video Game Makers."
Retrieved November 3, 2014 (http://www.ign.com
/top/video-game-makers).

Kamenetz, Anya. "Why Video Games Succeed Where
the Movie and Music Industries Fail." November
7, 2013. Retrieved November 4, 2014 (http://
www.fastcompany.com/3021008/why-video
-games-succeed-where-the-movie-and-music
-industries-fail).

Luckhurst, Phoebe. "Game Changers: The New
Female Power Players in the Video Gaming Industry." *London Evening Standard*, October 29, 2014.
Retrieved October 31, 2014 (http://www.standard
.co.uk/lifestyle/london-life/game-changers-the
-new-female-power-players-in-the-video-gaming
-industry-9825057.html).

Ohanesian, Liz. "Why Aren't There More Women
in the Video Game Industry?" *L.A. Weekly*, June
13, 2014. Retrieved October 30, 2014 (http://
www.laweekly.com/publicspectacle/2014/06
/13/why-arent-there-more-women-in-the-video
-game-industry).

Princeton Review. "Top Undergraduate Schools for
Video Game Design." Retrieved November 6, 2014

(http://www.princetonreview.com/top
-undergraduate-schools-for-video-game
-design.aspx).

Rose, Mike. "Exploring Video Game Animation with
a Film Industry Veteran." Gamasutra, April 4, 2013.
Retrieved November 10, 2014 (http://www
.gamasutra.com/view/news/189779/Exploring
_video_game_animation_with_a_film_industry
_veteran.php).

Suellentrop, Chris. "Saluting the Women Behind the
Screen." *New York Times,* August 19, 2014.
Retrieved November 18, 2014 (http://www
.nytimes.com/2014/08/20/arts/video-games
/those-underappreciated-female-video-game
-pioneers.html?_r=0).

Tassi, Paul. "Female Game Developers Have Doubled
Since 2009, Men Still Dominate Industry." *Forbes*,
June 25, 2014. Retrieved November 3, 2014 (http://
www.forbes.com/sites/insertcoin/2014/06/25/
female-game-developers-have-doubled-since
-2009-men-still-dominate-industry).

Thomas, Myra. "A Changing Job Market for Women in
Gaming." January 31, 2014. Retrieved October 31,
2014 (http://news.dice.com/2014/01/31/changing
-workplace-women-gaming).

U.S. News University Connection. "Computer Programming in the 21st Century—Video Game
Design Careers." 2012. Retrieved November 10,
2014 (http://www.usnewsuniversitydirectory.com/
articles/computer-programming-in-the-21st
-century-nda_12084.aspx#.VGDNh4fZfry).

Index

ABOUT THE AUTHOR

Laura La Bella learned to play video games as a young girl. She spent hours mastering *Pitfall!* and *BurgerTime* on her family's Atari 2600. In her spare time, when she's not raising her two sons or writing nonfiction children's books, she's on a quest to develop her kingdom in *Castleville Legends*. La Bella is also the reigning *Galaga* champion of her family.

PHOTO CREDITS

Cover © iStockphoto.com/stocknroll; cover and interior pages background image © iStockphoto.com/alengo; cover and interior pages text banners © iStockphoto.com/slav; p. 5 Paul Archuleta/Film Magic/Getty Images; p. 9 AE Pictures Inc./Digital Vision/Getty Images; p. 12 © AP Images; p. 15 Jim Wilson/The New York Times/Redux; p. 19 Heidi Schumann/The New York Times/Redux; p. 21 © Michael Goulding/The Orange County Register/ZUMA Press; p. 24 Lisa F. Young/Shutterstock.com; p. 27 Angela Weiss/WireImage/Getty Images; p. 29 Christopher Robbins/Digital Vision/Getty Images; p. 32 Thomas Barwick/Stone/Getty Images; p. 36 Mclek/Shutterstock.com; p. 38 scyther5/Shutterstock.com; p. 40 Xavier Popy/REA/Redux; p. 43 Barone Firenze/Shutterstock.com; pp. 44, 54 Bloomberg/Getty Images; p. 47 Joby Sessions/Computer Arts Magazine/Future/Getty Images; p. 49 Bob Ingelhart/E+/Getty Images; p. 51 Jon Feingerash/Iconica/Getty Images; p. 55 PeopleImages.com/Digital Vision/Getty Images; p. 63 Koene/Redux; p. 65 Carpe89/iStock Editorial/Thinkstock.

Designer: Nicole Russo; Editor: Tracey Baptiste